Doodle Dynamics
Dog Training for Doodle Breeds

Tyler Bradshaw

Horizon Publishing LLC

Please note the information contained within this document is for educational and entertainment purposes only. The author does not claim to be an expert or professional on the subject matter. All effort has been executed to present accurate, up to date, reliable, complete information. No warranties of any kind are declared or implied. Readers acknowledge that the author is not engaged in the rendering of legal, financial, medical or professional advice. The content within this book has been derived from various sources. Please consult a licensed professional before attempting any techniques outlined in this book.

By reading this document, the reader agrees that under no circumstances is the author responsible for any losses, direct or indirect, that are incurred as a result of the use of the information contained within this document, including, but not limited to, errors, omissions, or inaccuracies.

Table of Contents

Introduction

Doodle breeds, a cross between Poodles and various other dog breeds, have become increasingly popular over the past few decades. These hybrid dogs combine the intelligence, hypoallergenic coat, and trainability of a Poodle with the desirable traits of other breeds, resulting in a variety of Doodles such as the Labradoodle, Goldendoodle, Aussiedoodle, and Bernedoodle, among others.

- **Labradoodle**: A mix of Labrador Retriever and Poodle, known for its friendly, energetic, and social nature. Labradoodles are great family pets and excel in various roles, from therapy dogs to service animals.

- **Goldendoodle**: A cross between a Golden Retriever and a Poodle, Goldendoodles are playful, affectionate, and highly trainable. Due to their gentle nature, they are often seen as the best fit for a family dog.

- **Aussiedoodle**: A cross between an Australian Shepherd and a Poodle. Aussiedoodles are incredibly smart, loyal, and full of energy. They are well-liked because of their goofy and loving personalities. They are high energy, so they require a lot of exercise and activity, making them popular for active families.

- **Bernedoodle**: A blend of a Bernese Mountain Dog and a Poodle, Bernedoodles are known for their loyalty, calm demeanor, and striking appearance. They are excellent companions and can adapt well to different living environments.

Other popular Doodle breeds include the Yorkiepoo, Sheepadoodle, and Cavapoo, each bringing unique traits from their parent breeds. Regardless of the Doodle mix, these dogs generally share common characteristics such as intelligence, sociability, and a significant need for mental and physical stimulation.

Importance of Training

Training is vital for responsible dog ownership, particularly for intelligent and active breeds like Doodles. Proper training ensures your dog is well-behaved, safe, and a joy to be around. It also strengthens the bond between you and your pet, fostering a relationship built on trust and mutual respect.

Untrained dogs can develop behavioral problems that may lead to frustration for both the owner and the pet. These issues can range from minor annoyances like excessive barking to more serious problems like aggression or destructive behavior. Investing time and effort into training can prevent these issues and ensure your Doodle grows into a well-mannered and happy dog.

Setting Expectations

Before starting the training process, it's important to set realistic expectations. Training a dog, especially a young puppy, requires patience, consistency, and positive reinforcement. Understand that every dog learns at its own pace, and what works for one Doodle might not work for another. It's essential to be flexible and adjust your training methods as needed.

Training is not a one-time action but an ongoing process. Regular practice and reinforcement of commands and behaviors are necessary to maintain your dog's training. Additionally, training sessions should be fun and engaging for your Doodle.

Incorporate games, toys, and treats to keep your dog motivated and eager to learn.

This book provides detailed guidance on training your Doodle, from basic obedience to advanced techniques. Whether you're a first-time dog owner or an experienced handler, this guide will provide you with the tools and knowledge you need to successfully train your Doodle and build a strong, lasting bond.

What You Will Learn

- **Understanding Your Doodle**: Learn about the specific traits and characteristics of Doodle breeds and how these influence their training needs.

- **Puppy Training Basics**: Learn essential training techniques for your Doodle puppy, including house training, crate training, and socialization.

- **Basic Obedience Training**: Master fundamental commands such as sit, stay, and come, and learn how to leash train your dog effectively.

- **Advanced Training Techniques**: Explore more complex training methods, including off-leash training, recall, and advanced commands.

- **Addressing Behavioral Issues**: Identify common behavioral problems and discover strategies for addressing and correcting them using positive reinforcement.

- **Specialized Training for Doodles**: Dive into specialized training areas such as therapy and service dog training, agility training, and fun tricks.

- **Maintaining Training and Building a Bond**: Learn how to continue your dog's education, strengthen your relationship, and connect with the Doodle community for support and resources.

By the end of this book, you will have a comprehensive understanding of how to train your Doodle effectively, ensuring a well-behaved, happy, and healthy companion. Let's embark on this journey together and make training your Doodle an enjoyable and rewarding experience.

Chapter 1

Understanding Your Doodle

Traits and Characteristics

Doodle breeds, a cross between Poodles and various other dog breeds, are known for their friendly nature, intelligence, loyalty, and hypoallergenic coats. Each breed combines the best traits of their parent breeds, making them popular choices for families and individuals alike. Understanding the general characteristics of each breed can help you adjust your training approach to fit your dog's specific needs.

Behavioral Traits

Let's start by talking about some behavioral traits common to most all doodle dogs. They are generally highly intelligent and eager to please, making training both enjoyable and effective. However, their intelligence also means they can become easily bored and mischievous if not adequately stimulated. Providing a mix of mental and physical activities is essential to keep your doodle engaged and happy.

Socialization is also crucial for doodles, as they are typically sociable dogs that enjoy interacting with people and other animals. Early and consistent socialization helps prevent behavioral issues such as anxiety and aggression.

Health Considerations

Understanding the health considerations of your doodle breed is vital for their overall well-being. Doodles can inherit health issues from their parent breeds, so regular veterinary check-ups and a healthy diet are a must. Common health issues include hip dysplasia, allergies, and certain genetic conditions. Being proactive about your doodle's health will ensure they remain fit and active throughout their life.

Proper exercise is also essential for doodles, given their energetic nature. Regular walks, playtime, and opportunities to run and explore will keep them physically fit and mentally stimulated. Combining exercise with training sessions can make learning more effective and enjoyable for your doodle.

Popular Breeds

Labradoodle

Labradoodles are a cross between Labrador Retrievers and Poodles, and they have gained popularity for their friendly, outgoing nature and low-shedding coats. They come in three sizes: standard, medium, and miniature, depending on the size of the Poodle used in breeding.

- **Temperament**: Labradoodles are known for their friendly and social disposition. They tend to get along well with children and other pets, making them excellent family dogs. Their Labrador heritage gives them a love for play and outdoor activities, while the Poodle side contributes to their intelligence and trainability.

- **Appearance**: Labradoodles have a curly or wavy coat that is usually low-shedding, making them a popular choice for people with allergies. They come in a variety of colors, including cream, gold, chocolate, black, and parti (two colors).

- **Exercise Needs**: Labradoodles are active dogs that require regular exercise to keep them healthy and happy.

Daily walks, playtime, and mental stimulation through training and interactive toys are essential to meet their needs.

Goldendoodle

Goldendoodles are a mix between Golden Retrievers and Poodles, combining the best traits of both breeds. They are known for their friendly, affectionate nature and curly, hypoallergenic coats.

- **Temperament**: Goldendoodles are gentle, loving, and highly sociable dogs. They thrive on human interaction and are known for being great with children. Their intelligence and eagerness to please make them highly trainable, and they often excel in obedience training and canine sports.

- **Appearance**: Like Labradoodles, Goldendoodles have a curly or wavy coat that is typically low-shedding. They come in various colors, including cream, apricot, red, and black. Their coats require regular grooming to prevent matting and keep them looking their best.

- **Exercise Needs**: Goldendoodles are active and playful,

requiring daily exercise to stay healthy. Regular walks, play sessions, and opportunities to run and explore are essential to keep them physically and mentally stimulated.

Aussiedoodle

Aussiedoodles are a mix between Australian Shepherds and Poodles. They are known for their goofy playful nature but they are also highly intelligent and energetic.

- **Temperament**: Aussiedoodles are playful and fun-loving with affectionate personalities. They tend to be high-energy, requiring them to have a good amount of exercise and play to keep them mentally stimulated.

- **Appearance**: They have wavy, curly, medium-length hair that typically has little to moderate shedding. They come in several colors: black, brown, red, white, cream, gray, tan, merle, and combinations of more than one. They can weigh anywhere from 25-70 lbs. and be as tall as 10-15 inches.

- **Exercise Needs**: Aussiedoodles are active dogs that

need playtime and long walks every day. Their favorite activities include playing fetch, running, and swimming. They need at least an hour of movement daily to keep them happy and healthy.

Bernedoodle

Bernedoodles are a cross between Bernese Mountain Dogs and Poodles. They are known for their loyalty, calm demeanor, and striking appearance, often with a tri-color coat.

- **Temperament**: Bernedoodles are loyal and affectionate, forming strong bonds with their families. They tend to be more laid-back compared to other Doodle breeds, making them great companions for people looking for a more relaxed dog. However, they still require mental stimulation and enjoy learning new things.

- **Appearance**: Bernedoodles often have a wavy or curly coat that can be tri-colored (black, white, and brown), solid, or bi-colored. Their coats are usually low-shedding but require regular grooming to maintain.

- **Exercise Needs**: While Bernedoodles may be less energetic than Labradoodles or Goldendoodles, they still need regular exercise. Daily walks, playtime, and mental stimulation through training and puzzles are important to keep them happy and healthy.

Behavioral Traits

Understanding the behavioral traits of Doodle breeds is crucial for effective training. These traits are influenced by the characteristics of their parent breeds and can vary slightly depending on the specific mix.

- **Intelligence**: Doodles inherit high intelligence from their Poodle parents, making them quick learners. This trait is beneficial for training but also means they need mental stimulation to prevent boredom.

- **Sociability**: Most Doodles are naturally sociable and enjoy being around people and other animals. Early socialization is key to ensuring they grow up to be well-adjusted adults.

- **Energy Levels**: Doodles can have varying energy levels depending on their specific breed mix. Generally, they are active dogs that need regular exercise and playtime to stay happy and healthy.

- **Eagerness to Please**: Doodles are often eager to please their owners, which makes training easier. Positive reinforcement techniques work particularly well with these breeds.

Health Considerations

Like all breeds, Doodles can be prone to certain health issues inherited from their parent breeds. Regular veterinary check-ups, a healthy diet, and appropriate exercise are crucial for maintaining their health.

- **Hip Dysplasia**: This is common in larger breeds like Labradors and Bernese Mountain Dogs. Ensuring your Doodle maintains a healthy weight and gets regular, non-strenuous exercise can help mitigate this risk.

- **Allergies**: Some Doodles may develop allergies, manifesting as skin issues, itching, or gastrointestinal problems. A diet that avoids common allergens and regular grooming can help manage these conditions.

- **Genetic Conditions**: It's essential to work with reputable breeders who test for genetic conditions common in the parent breeds. Conditions such as progressive retinal atrophy (PRA) and von Willebrand's disease can be screened for before breeding.

- **Regular Exercise**: Ensuring your Doodle gets enough exercise is crucial for their physical and mental health. Regular walks, playtime, and opportunities for off-leash running in a safe area are essential for keeping them fit and happy.

Understanding your Doodle's breed characteristics, behavioral traits, and health considerations is the first step in successful training. Knowing what to expect and how to meet your dog's needs, can create a positive training environment that sets the stage for a well-behaved, happy, and healthy companion.

Chapter 2

Doodle Dos and Don'ts

Training Your Doodle Puppy

T raining your Doodle puppy is essential in ensuring they grow into a well-behaved and well-adjusted adult dog. This chapter will guide you through the fundamental aspects of puppy training, including house training, crate training, and socialization.

House Training

House training is often one of the first and most critical training tasks for a new puppy. It involves teaching your puppy where it's appropriate to go to the bathroom and establishing a routine that encourages good bathroom habits.

1. Establish a Routine

- **Consistent Feeding Schedule**: Feed your puppy at the same times each day. Consistent feeding schedules lead to predictable potty times.

- **Regular Bathroom Breaks**: Take your puppy outside frequently, especially after eating, drinking, playing, or waking up. Young puppies may need to go out every 30-60 minutes.

- **Designated Bathroom Area**: Choose a specific spot outside for your puppy to go to the bathroom. The scent will remind them that this is the right place to go.

2. Supervision and Confinement

- **Close Supervision**: Always keep a close eye on your puppy. Watch for signs that it needs to go out, such as sniffing, circling, or whining. The key to keeping things consistent is to catch their intentions before they go potty in the wrong place is the key to keeping things consistent.

- **Use of a Leash**: When taking your puppy outside, use a leash to guide them to the designated bathroom area and keep them focused. It may require patience at first, but stay persistent to establish a routine.

- **Crate Training**: Utilize a crate when you can't supervise your puppy. Dogs generally avoid soiling their sleeping area, so an appropriately sized crate can help with house training.

3. Positive Reinforcement

- **Praise and Rewards**: Immediately praise and reward your puppy with treats and affection after they eliminate in the appropriate spot. Positive reinforcement helps them associate good behavior with rewards. You could keep a small bag of treats next to the door or in your pocket so that you remember to have them on hand when they do their business in the place you intend them to go.

- **Consistency**: Be consistent with your commands and rewards. Use the same word or phrase each time you take your puppy out to encourage them to eliminate.

4. Handling Accidents

- **Stay Calm**: If your puppy has an accident, stay calm and do not punish them. Clean up any mess to remove any lingering odors that might attract them back to the same spot.

- **Reinforce Training**: If you catch your puppy in the act, gently interrupt them and take them outside immediately. Praise them if they finish eliminating outside.

Crate Training

Crate training is a valuable tool for house training and provides your puppy with a safe, comfortable space. When done correctly, crate training can help prevent destructive behavior and make travel and vet visits less stressful.

1. Choosing the Right Crate

- **Size**: Select a crate that is large enough for your puppy to stand, turn around, and lie down comfortably but not so large that they can go to the bathroom in one corner and sleep in another.

- **Type**: Crates are made of various materials, including wire, plastic, and fabric. Choose one that suits your puppy's needs and your lifestyle.

2. Introducing the Crate

- **Positive Association**: Make the crate a positive place by placing treats, toys, and comfortable bedding inside. Encourage your puppy to explore the crate voluntarily. You want to create comfort and safety for them in their crate space.

- **Gradual Introduction**: Start by opening the door of the crate and allowing your puppy to enter and exit freely. Gradually increase the amount of time they spend inside with the door closed. This will lessen their anxiety and allow them to get used to their new safe space.

3. Creating a Crate Routine

- **Short Periods**: Begin with brief periods in the crate, gradually increasing the time as your puppy becomes more comfortable.

- **Consistency**: Use the crate consistently for naps, overnight sleeping, and times when you can't supervise your puppy.

- **Avoid Using as Punishment**: Never use the crate as a form of punishment. It should always be a safe, positive space for your puppy.

Socialization

Socialization is the process of exposing your puppy to various people, places, sounds, other dogs, and experiences to help them become well-adjusted and confident adults. Early and consistent socialization is crucial for preventing behavioral problems and ensuring your puppy is comfortable in different environments and with other dogs.

1. Early Socialization

- **Critical Period**: The critical period for socialization is between 3 and 14 weeks of age. During this time, your puppy is most receptive to new experiences.

- **Safe Exposure**: Introduce your puppy to new people, animals, and environments in a controlled and positive manner. Ensure that all interactions are safe and positive. It's important to keep in mind that you should limit their exposure to other dogs or animals until they've had their first shots at the vet. This helps keep them safe from viruses they could catch when they're young and more vulnerable.

2. Exposure to Different Environments

- **Public Places**: Take your puppy to various public places, such as parks, dog-friendly stores, and outdoor cafes. Allow them to experience different sights, sounds, and smells.

- **Different Surfaces**: Expose your puppy to different surfaces like grass, gravel, concrete, and carpet. This helps them become comfortable walking on various textures.

3. Interaction with People and Animals

- **People**: Introduce your puppy to people of different ages, sizes, and ethnicities. Encourage gentle handling and positive interactions.

- **Other Dogs**: Arrange playdates with other vaccinated, friendly dogs. Supervised interactions help your puppy learn appropriate play behavior and social cues.

4. Handling and Grooming

- **Touch Sensitivity**: Regularly handle your puppy's paws, ears, tail, and mouth to get them used to being touched. This will make vet visits and grooming sessions less stressful.

- **Grooming Routines**: Introduce your puppy to grooming tools and routines early on. Brush their coat, trim their nails, and clean their ears regularly to keep them comfortable with the process.

Training your puppy can be a happy and stress-free experience when you are consistent and patient with your little one. Positive reinforcement and staying on top of the training techniques daily are the two most important things to ensure success. This is a time to set the groundwork for a lasting and loving bond with your new puppy.

Chapter 3

Basic Obedience Training

B asic obedience training ensures your Doodle becomes a well-behaved, manageable, and enjoyable companion. This chapter will guide you through the fundamental commands and techniques to establish a strong foundation of obedience, including sit, stay, come, leash training, and handling distractions.

Sit Command

The "sit" command is one of the easiest and most beneficial to teach your Doodle. It is the foundation for many other commands and behaviors.

1. How to Teach Sit

- **Starting Position**: Begin with your Doodle standing in front of you. Hold a treat close to their nose.

- **Luring**: Slowly move the treat upward and slightly back over your doodle's head. This motion should cause your Doodle to naturally lower it's hindquarters to the ground to follow the treat.

- **Command and Reward**: As soon as your Doodle's bottom touches the ground, say "Sit" and give them the treat, followed by lots of praise. Consistency and positive reinforcement are key.

2. Practice and Reinforcement

- **Short Sessions**: Practice in short, frequent sessions to keep your Doodle engaged and prevent frustration.

- **Consistency**: Use the same command and hand signal each time. Consistency helps your Doodle understand what is expected of them.

- **Gradual Reduction of Treats**: Gradually reduce the frequency of treats over time, replacing them with words of praise and petting. This helps your Doodle learn to respond without expecting a treat every time.

Stay Command

The "stay" command is crucial for teaching your Doodle self-control and patience. It is helpful in various situations, such as preventing them from bolting out the door or staying calm during vet visits.

1. How to Teach Stay

- **Starting Position**: Begin with your Doodle in a sitting position. Hold your hand out, palm facing them, as a signal to stay.

- **Command and Duration**: Say "Stay" and take a small step back. If your Doodle remains in place, step forward and reward them with a treat and praise.

- **Gradual Increase**: Gradually increase the duration and distance of the stay command. Start with a few seconds and slowly work up to longer periods and greater distances.

2. Practice and Reinforcement

- **Consistency**: Be consistent with your hand signal and verbal command. Use a calm, firm tone.

- **Return to Reward**: Always return to your Doodle to reward them for staying in place, rather than calling them to you. This reinforces the idea that "stay" means to remain where they are.

- **Distractions**: Once your Doodle reliably stays in a quiet environment, introduce mild distractions and gradually increase the difficulty. This helps them learn to stay focused even in busy settings.

Come Command

The "come" command, or recall, is essential for your Doodle's safety. A reliable recall ensures your dog returns to you promptly, even in distracting or potentially dangerous situations.

1. How to Teach Come

- **Starting Position**: Begin in a safe, enclosed area. Use a long leash if necessary.

- **Encouragement**: Say "Come" in a happy, enthusiastic tone while gently pulling the leash or running backward to encourage your Doodle to follow you.

- **Reward**: When your Doodle reaches you, praise them

enthusiastically and give them a treat. Make coming to you a positive experience.

2. Practice and Reinforcement

- **Short Distances**: Start with short distances and gradually increase as your Doodle becomes more reliable.

- **Varied Locations**: Practice in different locations and environments to ensure your Doodle responds to the command regardless of where they are.

- **Avoid Negative Associations**: Never call your Doodle to you for something they might perceive as negative, such as a bath or scolding. This could make them hesitant to come when called.

Leash Training

Leash training is vital for enjoyable and safe walks with your Doodle. Proper leash manners prevent pulling and other undesirable behaviors.

1. How to Teach Leash Walking

- **Starting Indoors**: To minimize distractions, begin

leash training indoors or in a quiet, familiar area. Attach the leash to your Doodle's collar or harness.

- **Loose Leash**: Hold the leash loosely, allowing some slack. Start walking and use a happy, encouraging tone to keep your Doodle focused on you.

- **Reward for Position**: Reward your Doodle with treats and praise when they walk beside you with a loose leash. This reinforces the desired behavior.

2. Addressing Pulling

- **Stop and Stand Still**: If your Doodle starts to pull, stop walking immediately. Stand still and wait for them to return to your side. Reward them when they do.

- **Change Direction**: Alternatively, change direction when your Doodle pulls. This teaches them that pulling does not get them where they want to go.

- **Consistency**: Be consistent with your responses to pulling. Avoid letting your Doodle pull you, as this reinforces the behavior.

Handling Distractions

Teaching your Doodle to stay focused and obey commands even in distracting environments is essential for reliable obedience.

1. Gradual Exposure

- **Controlled Environments**: Start training in a controlled environment with minimal distractions. Gradually introduce mild distractions as your Doodle becomes more proficient with the commands.

- **Increase Difficulty**: Slowly increase the level of distraction by practicing in busier areas, such as parks or near other dogs. Reward your Doodle for maintaining focus and obeying commands.

2. Use of High-Value Rewards

- **Special Treats**: Use high-value treats that your Doodle finds particularly motivating when training in distracting environments. This increases their incentive to stay focused on you.

- **Toys and Play**: Incorporate your Doodle's favorite toys or play sessions as rewards for good behavior. This keeps training fun and engaging.

3. Patience and Consistency

- **Short Sessions**: Keep training sessions short and positive to prevent frustration and keep your Doodle engaged.

- **Repetition**: Consistent practice in various settings helps your Doodle generalize commands and understand that they must obey regardless of the environment.

Practical Tips and Troubleshooting

Training isn't always straightforward, and you may encounter challenges along the way. Here are some practical tips and solutions to common issues you might face during basic obedience training.

1. Dealing with Stubbornness

- **Patience**: Some Doodles may take longer to grasp specific commands. Be patient and avoid getting frustrated.

- **Break it Down**: Break the command into smaller steps and reward your Doodle for each small achievement.

- **Short, Frequent Sessions**: Keep training sessions short to prevent boredom and frustration. Frequent, shorter sessions can be more effective than long ones.

2. Overcoming Distraction Challenges

- **High-Value Rewards**: Use especially tasty treats or favorite toys to keep your Doodle's attention.

- **Training Aids**: Consider using training aids like clickers or treat pouches to make rewarding easier and more immediate.

- **Controlled Environments**: Start training in low-distraction environments and gradually introduce more distractions as your Doodle becomes more reliable.

3. Consistency is Key

- **Everyone on Board**: Ensure all family members use the same commands and training methods to avoid confusing your Doodle.

- **Regular Practice**: Consistent, daily practice is essential for reinforcing commands and behaviors.

4. Positive Reinforcement

- **Encouragement**: Always use positive reinforcement methods, such as treats, praise, and play, to encourage good behavior.

- **Avoid Punishment**: Avoid using punishment or negative reinforcement, as this can lead to fear and anxiety, hindering training progress.

Basic obedience training lays the groundwork for a well-behaved and manageable Doodle. By mastering commands such as sit, stay, come, and proper leash manners and teaching your Doodle to handle distractions, you set the stage for more advanced training and a happy dog-to-human relationship. Remember, patience, consistency, and positive reinforcement are the keys to successful training. The next chapter, will delve into advanced training techniques to further enhance your Doodle's skills and obedience.

Chapter 4

Advanced Training Techniques

Once your Doodle has mastered basic obedience commands, it's time to move on to more advanced training techniques. These advanced skills enhance your dog's obedience and manners, provide mental stimulation, and strengthen the bond between you and your Doodle. This chapter covers advanced training methods, including off-leash training, recall, and advanced commands.

Off-Leash Training

Training your Doodle to be reliable off-leash is an invaluable skill. It provides them more freedom while ensuring their safety. Off-leash training requires a solid foundation in basic obedience, particularly a strong recall command.

1. Preparation

- **Reliable Recall**: Ensure your Doodle has a reliable

recall command before attempting off-leash training. Practice recall consistently in various environments and with increasing distractions.

- **Safe Environment**: Start in a secure, enclosed area such as a fenced yard or an empty, enclosed park. Gradually move to more open spaces as your Doodle becomes more reliable.

2. Steps for Off-Leash Training

- **Long Leash Training**: Begin with a long leash or a retractable leash. This gives your Doodle a sense of freedom while allowing you to maintain control.

- **Gradual Freedom**: Gradually increase the length of the leash, allowing more freedom as your Doodle demonstrates reliability.

- **Off-Leash in Controlled Area**: Once your Doodle consistently responds to commands on the long leash, try off-leash training in a controlled, secure environment.

- **Recall Practice**: Call your Doodle back to you, rewarding them with high-value treats or praise. This reinforces the recall command and makes returning to you a positive experience.

3. Tips for Success

- **Stay Engaged**: Keep your Doodle engaged by changing direction frequently, playing games, and offering treats or toys. This encourages them to pay attention to you.

- **Avoid Negative Associations**: Never call your Doodle to you for something they perceive as unfavorable, such as ending playtime or leaving the park. This can make them hesitant to come when called.

- **Patience and Consistency**: Off-leash training takes time and patience. Be consistent with your training and consistently reinforce positive behavior.

Advanced Recall

A strong recall is crucial for your Doodle's safety, especially in off-leash situations. Advanced recall training builds on the basic recall command, enhancing reliability even with high distractions.

1. Proofing Recall

- **Increasing Distractions**: Practice recall in various environments with increasing distractions, such as parks, near other dogs, or busy areas.

- **High-Value Rewards**: Use high-value rewards that your Doodle finds particularly motivating. This increases their incentive to respond quickly.

- **Random Recall**: Call your Doodle randomly during playtime or walks, rewarding them generously for responding. This teaches them that coming to you can happen anytime and is always rewarding.

2. Emergency Recall

- **Unique Command**: Choose a unique, distinct command for emergency recall, such as "Here" or "Now," that differs from the regular recall command.

- **High-Value Reward**: Use your highest-value rewards, such as a favorite treat or toy, to reinforce the emergency recall command.

- **Practice in a Controlled Environment**: Start practicing in a controlled environment with minimal distractions, gradually increasing the difficulty as your Doodle responds reliably.

Advanced Commands

Teaching advanced commands enhances your Doodle's obedience and mental stimulation. These commands can include complex behaviors, tricks, and specialized tasks.

1. Advanced Commands to Teach

- **Heel**: Teaching your Doodle to walk beside you without pulling. Use a command like "Heel" and reward them for staying close to your side.

- **Place**: Training your Doodle to go to a designated spot, such as a mat or bed, and stay there until released.

- **Leave It**: Teach your Doodle to ignore or move away from an object or distraction. Start with low-value items and gradually increase the difficulty.

- **Fetch and Drop It**: Teach your Doodle to fetch and bring an item back to you, releasing it on command.

2. Steps for Teaching Advanced Commands

- **Break Down the Behavior**: Break the behavior into

small, manageable steps. Reward your Doodle for each step toward the final behavior.

- **Consistent Cues**: Use consistent verbal and hand cues for each command. Consistency helps your Doodle understand and respond to the commands.

- **Gradual Increase in Difficulty**: Gradually increase the difficulty of the command, such as increasing the duration or introducing distractions.

3. Tips for Advanced Training

- **Positive Reinforcement**: Always use positive reinforcement methods, such as treats, praise, and play, to encourage good behavior.

- **Short, Frequent Sessions**: Keep training sessions short and frequent to maintain your Doodle's interest and prevent frustration.

- **Practice in Various Environments**: Practice commands in different locations and environments to ensure your Doodle can generalize the behavior and respond reliably in any situation.

Agility and Fun Activities

Incorporating agility training and fun activities into your Doodle's routine provides physical exercise and mental stimulation, enhancing their overall well-being.

1. Agility Training

- **Fundamental Obstacles**: Start with primary obstacles like tunnels, jumps, and weave poles. Use treats and praise to guide your Doodle through each obstacle.

- **Gradual Progression**: Gradually increase the difficulty and complexity of the agility course as your Doodle becomes more proficient.

- **Positive Reinforcement**: Use positive reinforcement to encourage and reward your Doodle for completing each obstacle.

2. Fun Activities

- **Hide and Seek**: Play hide and seek with your Doodle, hiding treats or toys for them to find. This engages their natural scenting and hunting instincts.

- **Interactive Toys**: Use interactive toys like puzzle feeders or treat-dispensing toys to provide mental stimulation and keep your Doodle engaged.

- **Trick Training**: Teach fun tricks such as "Roll Over," "Spin," or "Shake." These tricks provide mental exercise and can be a fun way to bond with your Doodle.

Advanced training techniques not only enhance your Doodle's obedience and manners but also provide necessary mental stimulation and physical exercise. By mastering off-leash training, advanced recall, and complex commands, you can ensure your Doodle is well-behaved, engaged, and happy. Remember, patience, consistency, and positive reinforcement are essential to successful training. The next chapter will address common behavioral issues and provide strategies to correct and manage them effectively.

Chapter 5

Addressing Behavioral Issues

B ehavioral issues can be frustrating for dog owners, but they are a natural part of owning a pet. Addressing these issues early on with positive reinforcement strategies is crucial for preventing them from becoming habits. This chapter will cover common behavioral problems in Doodles, including barking, chewing, digging, and separation anxiety, and provide strategies to correct and manage these behaviors effectively.

Common Behavioral Problems

1. Barking

Barking is a natural form of communication for dogs, but excessive barking can become a problem. Understanding the reasons behind your Doodle's barking is the first step in addressing this behavior.

- **Attention-Seeking Barking**: If your Doodle barks to

get your attention, they have learned that barking results in a response from you.

- **Alert Barking**: Doodles may bark to alert you to perceived threats or unfamiliar sounds. This type of barking is common in many dogs.

- **Boredom or Anxiety**: Barking can also be a sign of boredom or anxiety, particularly if your Doodle is left alone for long periods.

Strategies to Address Barking

- **Ignore Attention-Seeking Barking**: Do not respond to your Doodle's barking if it is attention-seeking. Wait for a moment of silence before giving attention or rewards.

- **Desensitize to Triggers**: Gradually expose your Doodle to the sounds or situations that trigger barking, rewarding them for remaining quiet.

- **Provide Mental and Physical Stimulation**: Ensure your Doodle gets plenty of exercise and mental stimulation to prevent boredom-related barking.

- **Teach a Quiet Command**: Use a command such as "Quiet" and reward your Doodle for stopping barking. This positive reinforcement helps to keep your Doodle eager to please.

2. Chewing

Chewing is a natural behavior for dogs, especially puppies, but it can become problematic if your Doodle chews on inappropriate items.

- **Teething**: Puppies chew to relieve the discomfort of teething.

- **Boredom or Anxiety**: Chewing can also indicate boredom or anxiety in adult dogs. It may also indicate that your dog isn't receiving adequate exercise or activity. Keeping your dog active and engaged can help reduce anxiety and increase their overall happiness.

Strategies to Address Chewing

- **Provide Appropriate Chew Toys**: Offer a variety of chew toys to satisfy your Doodle's need to chew. Rotate toys to keep them interesting.

- **Puppy-Proof Your Home**: Remove or secure items you don't want your Doodle to chew on.

- **Supervise and Redirect**: Supervise your Doodle and redirect their chewing to appropriate toys if you catch them chewing on inappropriate items.

- **Use Deterrents**: Apply taste deterrents to items you don't want your Doodle to chew.

3. Digging

Digging is another natural behavior for dogs, but it can become problematic if your Doodle digs in inappropriate areas.

- **Instinctual Behavior**: Some dogs dig to create a cool spot to lie in or to hide food and toys.

- **Boredom or Anxiety**: Digging can also signify boredom or anxiety.

Strategies to Address Digging

- **Provide a Designated Digging Area**: Create a designated area in your yard and encourage your Doodle to dig there by burying toys or treats.

- **Exercise and Mental Stimulation**: Ensure your Doodle gets plenty of exercise and mental stimulation to prevent boredom-related digging.

- **Supervise and Redirect**: Supervise your Doodle and redirect their digging to the designated area if you catch them digging in inappropriate places.

4. Separation Anxiety

Separation anxiety is a common issue in Doodles, characterized by distress and problematic behaviors when left alone.

- **Signs of Separation Anxiety**: Signs include excessive barking, whining, destructive behavior, and house soiling when you leave.

- **Causes**: Separation anxiety can be triggered by changes in routine, moving to a new home, or a lack of proper socialization.

Strategies to Address Separation Anxiety

- **Gradual Desensitization**: Gradually get your Doodle used to being alone by leaving them for short periods and gradually increasing the duration.

- **Create a Safe Space**: Provide a comfortable, safe space with toys and treats where your Doodle can relax when you're not home.

- **Consistent Routine**: Maintain a consistent leave and return home routine to reduce anxiety.

- **Interactive Toys and Puzzles**: Provide interactive toys and puzzles to keep your Doodle occupied while you're away.

- **Professional Help**: In severe cases, consider seeking help from a professional dog trainer or behaviorist.

Positive Reinforcement Strategies

Positive reinforcement is the most effective and humane method for addressing behavioral issues in dogs. This approach focuses on rewarding desirable behaviors rather than punishing unwanted ones.

1. Understanding Positive Reinforcement

- **Timing**: Reward your Doodle immediately after they perform the desired behavior. This helps them make the connection between the behavior and the reward.

- **Consistency**: Be consistent with your rewards. Every time your Doodle performs the desired behavior, they should receive a reward.

- **Variety of Rewards**: To keep your Doodle motivated, you can reward them with treats, praise, and toys.

2. Implementing Positive Reinforcement

- **Identify the Behavior**: Identify the behavior you want to encourage. For example, if you wish to reduce barking, reward your Doodle when they are quiet.

- **Use a Marker**: Use a marker, such as a clicker or a verbal cue like "Yes," to signal to your Doodle that they have performed the desired behavior and a reward is coming.

- **Reward Appropriately**: Choose rewards that your Doodle finds motivating. High-value treats or favorite toys are often effective.

3. Addressing Specific Behaviors with Positive Reinforcement

- **Barking**: Use a quiet command and reward your Doodle for being silent. Gradually increase the duration they need to be calm before receiving a reward.

- **Chewing**: Provide appropriate chew toys and reward your Doodle for chewing on them. Redirect their attention if they start chewing on inappropriate items.

- **Digging**: Encourage your Doodle to dig in a designated area and reward them. Redirect their digging to the appropriate spot if necessary.

- **Separation Anxiety**: Reward your Doodle for calm behavior when you leave and return. Gradually increase the time they spend alone, rewarding them for staying calm.

Consistency and Patience

Addressing behavioral issues takes time and patience. Consistency in your approach is key to success.

1. Be Patient

- **Progress Takes Time**: Behavioral changes don't happen overnight. Be patient and give your Doodle time to learn and adapt.

- **Small Steps**: Focus on small, incremental changes rather than expecting immediate results.

2. Stay Consistent

- **Same Commands and Cues**: Use the same commands and cues consistently to avoid confusing your Doodle.

- **Regular Training Sessions**: Schedule regular training sessions to reinforce desired behaviors and prevent regression.

3. Monitor Progress

- **Keep a Journal**: Keep a journal of your Doodle's progress, noting any improvements or setbacks. This can help you identify patterns and adjust your training approach if needed.

- **Celebrate Successes**: Celebrate small successes and milestones in your Doodle's behavior. Positive reinforcement applies to both you and your dog!

Addressing behavioral issues in your Doodle requires understanding, patience, and consistent positive reinforcement. By identifying the root causes of behaviors such as barking, chewing, digging, and separation anxiety and implementing effective strategies, you can help your Doodle become a well-behaved and happy companion. In the next chapter, we will explore specialized training for Doodles, including therapy and service dog training, agility training, and fun tricks and activities.

Chapter 6

Specialized Training for Doodles

D oodles are beloved family pets and excel in various specialized roles due to their intelligence, trainability, and friendly nature. This chapter will delve into specialized training areas such as therapy and service dog training, agility training, and teaching fun tricks and activities to mentally and physically stimulate your Doodle.

Therapy and Service Dog Training

Training a Doodle as a therapy or service dog involves rigorous training and a specific temperament. These roles require a calm demeanor, excellent obedience, and reliably performing tasks.

1. Understanding the Roles

- **Therapy Dogs**: Therapy dogs provide emotional support and comfort in settings such as hospitals, nursing homes, schools, and disaster areas. They must be well-behaved, gentle, and enjoy interacting with people.

- **Service Dogs**: Service dogs assist individuals with disabilities by performing specific tasks to enhance their independence. Tasks can include guiding visually impaired individuals, alerting them to medical conditions, or retrieving items.

2. Key Traits for Therapy and Service Dogs

- **Calm Temperament**: Dogs must remain calm and composed in various environments and situations.

- **Excellent Obedience**: Strong obedience skills are crucial, as therapy and service dogs must follow commands reliably.

- **Socialization**: Working to socialize your doodle often ensures that the dog is comfortable around different people, animals, and environments.

3. Steps for Training Therapy and Service Dogs

- **Basic Obedience**: Master basic commands such as sit, stay, come, and heel. Consistent obedience is the foundation of therapy and service dog training.

- **Public Access Training**: Gradually expose your Doodle to public environments where they will work, such as stores, public transportation, and crowded areas. Train them to remain calm and focused despite distractions.

- **Task Training**: For service dogs, train specific tasks tailored to the individual's needs. This could include retrieving items, opening doors, or alerting to medical conditions.

- **Certification and Testing**: Many organizations offer certification for therapy dogs, which involves passing a series of tests to ensure they meet the necessary standards. Service dogs may also undergo evaluations to ensure they can perform their tasks reliably.

4. Resources and Support

- **Professional Trainers**: Working with skilled trainers who specialize in therapy and service dog training can provide valuable guidance and support.

- **Therapy and Service Dog Organizations**: Organizations such as Therapy Dogs International (TDI) and Assistance Dogs International (ADI) offer resources, certification programs, and support for handlers and their dogs.

Agility Training

Agility training is an exciting and engaging activity that provides physical exercise and mental stimulation for your Doodle. It involves navigating an obstacle course with various challenges, such as jumps, tunnels, weave poles, etc.

1. Benefits of Agility Training

- **Physical Exercise**: Agility training provides a great workout, helping to keep your Doodle fit and healthy.

- **Mental Stimulation**: Navigating the obstacles and following your commands challenges your Doodle's mind and helps prevent boredom.

- **Bonding**: Working together on agility courses strengthens the bond between you and your Doodle.

2. Getting Started with Agility Training

- **Basic Obedience**: Ensure your Doodle has a solid foundation in basic obedience commands, which are essential for agility training.

- **Introduce Obstacles**: Start with simple obstacles such as tunnels, jumps, and weave poles. Use treats and praise to encourage your Doodle to navigate each obstacle.

- **Positive Reinforcement**: Reward your Doodle for successfully completing obstacles and following your commands. Keep training sessions fun and positive.

- **Increase Difficulty Gradually**: As your Doodle becomes more confident and skilled, gradually increase the difficulty and complexity of the agility courses.

3. Agility Equipment

- **Jumps**: Set up various types of jumps, such as bar jumps, tire jumps, and broad jumps. Adjust the height according to your Doodle's size and skill level.

- **Tunnels**: Use open or closed tunnels to teach your Doodle to run through. Start with a short, straight tunnel and gradually increase the length and add curves.

- **Weave Poles**: Introduce weave poles by guiding your Doodle through them with treats. Start with a few poles and gradually add more as they improve.

- **Contact Obstacles**: Contact obstacles like A-frames, dog walks, and teeter-totters require your Doodle to walk up and down ramps. Teach them to touch specific points to ensure safety and precision.

4. Joining an Agility Club

- **Local Clubs**: Joining a local agility club can provide access to equipment, training sessions, and competitions. It's also a great way to meet other dog enthusiasts and gain support.

- **Competitions**: Participating in agility competitions can be a fun way to challenge your Doodle and showcase their skills. Many clubs host trials and events for various skill levels.

Tricks and Fun Activities

Teaching your Doodle tricks and engaging in fun activities keeps training enjoyable and provides mental and physical stimulation.

1. Fun Tricks to Teach

- **Shake Hands:** Teach your Doodle to offer their paw on command. Start by lifting their paw and giving a treat, then add the verbal cue "Shake."

- **Roll Over:** With your Doodle in a lying down position, use a treat to guide them into rolling over. Reward them when they complete the roll.

- **Spin:** Hold a treat in front of your Doodle's nose and move it in a circle to encourage them to spin. Add the verbal cue "Spin" and reward them for following the treat.

- **Play Dead:** Teach your Doodle to lie on their side and stay still on command. Use a treat to guide them into the position and add the cue "Play Dead."

2. Interactive Games

- **Hide and Seek**: Hide treats or toys around your home or yard and encourage your Doodle to find them. This engages their natural scenting and hunting instincts.

- **Fetch**: Play fetch with a ball or toy. This provides physical exercise and reinforces the "Come" command.

- **Tug-of-War**: Play tug-of-war with a sturdy toy. This is a great way to bond with your Doodle and provide physical exercise.

3. Mental Stimulation

- **Puzzle Toys**: Use puzzle toys that dispense treats as your Doodle solves them. These toys provide mental exercise and keep your Doodle occupied.

- **Training Sessions**: Regular training sessions that include new tricks and commands keep your Doodle's mind active and engaged.

- **Interactive Play**: Engage in interactive play sessions that challenge your Doodle to think and solve problems. This can include games like "Find It," where you hide a toy and have your Doodle search for it.

Specialized training for Doodles, including therapy and service dog training, agility training, and fun tricks and activities, enhances their mental and physical well-being. By exploring these advanced training areas, you can provide your Doodle with the stimulation they need while strengthening your bond and having fun together. Remember to use positive reinforcement, be patient, and keep training sessions enjoyable. In the final chapter, we will discuss maintaining training, building a strong bond with your Doodle, and connecting with the community and resources for ongoing support.

Chapter 7

Maintaining Training and Building a Bond

T raining your Doodle doesn't end once they have mastered basic and advanced commands. It's a lifelong process that helps maintain good behavior, reinforces the human-dog bond, and stimulates your Doodle mentally and physically. This chapter will cover how to continue your Doodle's education, strengthen your relationship, and connect with the community for support and resources.

Continuing Education

1. Regular Training Sessions

- **Short and Frequent**: To maintain your Doodle's interest and engagement, keep training sessions short (5-10 minutes) and frequent. Daily sessions are ideal.

- **Incorporate into Daily Routine**: Use everyday opportunities to reinforce commands and teach new behaviors. For example, ask your Doodle to sit before meals or to wait in the doorways.

- **Advanced Training Classes**: Enroll in advanced training classes or workshops to learn new techniques and skills. These classes provide structured learning and socialization opportunities.

2. Introducing New Commands and Tricks

- **Keep It Fun**: Continuously introduce new commands and tricks to keep training exciting. This prevents boredom and keeps your Doodle mentally stimulated.

- **Challenge Their Intelligence**: Doodles are intelligent dogs that thrive on learning new things. Challenge them with complex commands, problem-solving tasks, and interactive toys.

- **Positive Reinforcement**: Continue using positive reinforcement to encourage good behavior. Reward your Doodle with treats, praise, and play for their achievements.

3. Reinforcing Old Commands

- **Consistency**: Regularly practice old commands to ensure your Doodle retains them. Consistency is vital to maintaining reliable behavior.

- **Varying Environments**: Practice commands to generalize the behavior in different environments and situations. This helps your Doodle respond reliably regardless of the setting.

- **Use in Real-Life Scenarios**: Apply commands in real-life scenarios, such as calling your Doodle to you during a walk or asking them to stay while you answer the door.

Strengthening the Human-Dog Relationship

1. Quality Time Together

- **Daily Interaction**: Spend quality time with your Doodle every day. This can include walks, playtime, grooming, or simply cuddling on the couch.

- **Active Play**: Engage in active play sessions that both you and your Doodle enjoy. This can include fetch, tug-of-war, or agility training.

- **Bonding Activities**: Participate in bonding activities such as hiking, swimming, or visiting dog-friendly parks and events.

2. Understanding Your Doodle's Needs

- **Physical Exercise**: Ensure your Doodle gets enough exercise to meet their energy needs. This helps prevent behavioral issues and keeps them healthy.

- **Mental Stimulation**: Provide mental stimulation through training, puzzle toys, and interactive play. A mentally stimulated Doodle is a happy and well-behaved Doodle.

- **Health and Wellness**: Regular veterinary check-ups, a balanced diet, and proper grooming are essential for your Doodle's overall health and well-being.

3. Building Trust and Communication

- **Positive Interactions**: Focus on positive interactions and avoid punishment-based training methods. Building trust is crucial for a strong, healthy relationship.

- **Clear Communication**: Use clear and consistent cues and commands. Understanding your Doodle's body language and signals also enhances communication.

- **Patience and Empathy**: Be patient and empathetic towards your Doodle's needs and limitations. Each dog learns at their own pace, and understanding this helps build a stronger bond.

Community and Resources

1. Joining Dog Training Groups and Clubs

- **Local Training Clubs**: Join local dog training clubs to meet other dog owners, share stories and experiences, and participate in group training sessions.

- **Online Communities**: Participate in online forums and social media groups dedicated to Doodle owners and dog training. These communities offer valuable advice, support, and resources.

2. Continuing Education for Owners

- **Workshops and Seminars**: Attend workshops and seminars on dog training and behavior to stay updated on the latest techniques and knowledge.

- **Books and Online Courses**: Invest in books and online courses to deepen your understanding of dog training and behavior. Continuous learning helps you become a better trainer and owner.

3. Professional Support

- **Dog Trainers and Behaviorists**: Seek help from professional dog trainers and behaviorists if you encounter specific challenges or need personalized guidance.

- **Veterinarians**: Regular veterinary visits are crucial for monitoring your Doodle's health and addressing medical or behavioral concerns.

4. Participating in Dog-Friendly Events

- **Dog Shows and Competitions**: Participate in or attend dog shows, agility competitions, and obedience trials. These events provide opportunities to showcase your Doodle's skills and socialize with other dog enthusiasts.

- **Community Events**: Join local dog-friendly community events such as dog walks, charity runs, and pet fairs. These events are great for socialization and bonding with your Doodle.

Maintaining Training and Behavior

1. Addressing Behavioral Changes

- **Monitor Behavior**: Regularly monitor your Doodle's behavior for any changes. Address issues quickly to prevent them from becoming habits.

- **Adjust Training Methods**: Be flexible and adjust your training methods as needed. Each dog is unique, and what works for one may not work for another.

- **Seek Professional Help**: If you experience persistent behavioral issues, don't hesitate to seek help from a professional trainer or behaviorist.

2. Reinforcement and Consistency

- **Regular Practice**: Regularly practice commands and behaviors to reinforce training. Consistency is key to maintaining good behavior.

- **Positive Reinforcement**: Continue using positive reinforcement to reward good behavior. This encourages your Doodle to repeat desired behaviors.

3. Creating a Positive Environment

- **Enrichment Activities**: Provide enrichment activities to keep your Doodle engaged and happy. This includes interactive toys, puzzle feeders, and sensory experiences.

- **Safe and Comfortable Space**: Ensure your Doodle has a safe and comfortable space where they can relax and feel secure.

Maintaining training and building a strong bond with your Doodle is an ongoing process that requires time, patience, and commitment. You can ensure a happy, healthy, and well-behaved companion by continuing education, understanding your Doodle's needs, and staying connected with the community and resources. Remember, the journey of training and bonding with your Doodle is a rewarding experience that strengthens your relationship and enhances your dog's quality of life.

Chapter 8

Conclusion

Your Doodle and You

I n this book, we've covered the essentials of Doodle training, from understanding their unique traits to mastering
advanced commands and addressing behavioral issues. With
the right approach, positive reinforcement, and a strong bond,
you can enjoy a fulfilling and harmonious life with your Doodle.

Training a Doodle is a journey filled with love, patience, and
mutual learning. From understanding the unique traits of your
Doodle breed to mastering basic and advanced commands,
every step you take together strengthens the bond between
you and your beloved companion. This book has guided you
through the essential aspects of training, from the basics of
house training and socialization to the intricacies of advanced
obedience and specialized training. You can revisit any chapters
for technique reminders and to help solidify training. Here is an
overview of what we just covered:

Understanding Your Doodle: By delving into different Doodle breeds' characteristics and behavioral traits, you've gained valuable insights into what makes your dog tick. Recognizing their intelligence, sociability, and exercise needs sets the foundation for a successful training experience.

Building the Basics: The fundamentals of puppy training, such as house training, crate training, and socialization, are crucial first steps. These early lessons pave the way for a well-adjusted, confident adult dog capable of navigating various environments and situations with ease.

Mastering Obedience: Basic obedience commands like sit, stay, come, and proper leash manners form the cornerstone of good behavior. Consistency, positive reinforcement, and patience have been your allies in teaching these essential skills.

Advancing Skills: Moving beyond the basics, advanced training techniques, such as off-leash training and recall, not only enhance your Doodle's obedience but also provide them with mental stimulation and freedom. Agility training and fun tricks keep your Doodle engaged, challenged, and happy.

Addressing Challenges: Every dog faces behavioral issues at some point. By understanding common problems like barking, chewing, and separation anxiety and addressing them with positive reinforcement strategies, you've learned to guide your Doodle toward better behavior while maintaining a loving and supportive environment.

Specialized Training: Whether training your Doodle as a therapy or service dog or exploring the world of agility, these specialized roles highlight the incredible potential and versatility of Doodle breeds. They show that with the proper training, your Doodle can excel in various fields, providing comfort, assistance, and joy to those around them.

Maintaining and Strengthening the Bond: Training doesn't end; it's a lifelong commitment to your Doodle's education and well-being. By continuing training, spending quality time together, and staying connected with the community, you ensure your Doodle remains well-behaved, happy, and healthy. This ongoing process reinforces the bond you share and enriches your lives together.

The journey of training your Doodle is not just about teaching commands and correcting behavior; it's about building a deep, trusting relationship that brings joy and companionship. Your dedication, patience, and love are the keys to unlocking your Doodle's potential and fostering a lifelong bond.

As you continue this journey, remember that each step you take together is a testament to the enduring bond between human and dog. Celebrate the successes, learn from the challenges, and cherish the moments of joy and companionship. Your Doodle is not just a pet; they are a beloved member of your family, and your commitment to their training and well-being reflects your love and care for them.

Thank you for embarking on this journey with your Doodle. May your days be filled with wagging tails, playful moments, and a bond that grows stronger with each passing day. Happy training, and may you and your Doodle enjoy a lifetime of happiness and companionship.

Made in the USA
Thornton, CO
01/01/25 13:45:09

590ec841-2cc4-417c-9102-56c5bf644bacR01